Ripley's Believe It or Not!®

REPTILES, LIZARDS AND PREHISTORIC BEASTS

A Byron Preiss Book

A Tom Doherty Associates Book
New York

RL 4.8 IL 011-013

The Ripley's 100th Anniversary Series:

Weird Inventions and Discoveries
Odd Places
Strange Coincidences
Wild Animals
Reptiles, Lizards and Prehistoric Beasts
Great and Strange Works of Man

Ripley's Believe It or Not!
Reptiles, Lizards and Prehistoric Beasts

Copyright © 1992 by Ripley Entertainment Inc.
Trademarks owned by Ripley Entertainment Inc.
Cover design by Dean Motter
Interior design by William Mohalley
Edited by Howard Zimmerman and Elizabeth Henderson

A TOR Book
Published by Tom Doherty Associates, Inc.
175 Fifth Avenue
New York, New York 10010

Tor® is a registered trademark of Tom Doherty Associates, Inc.

ISBN: 0-812-51290-1

First Tor edition: December 1992

Printed in the United States of America

0 9 8 7 6 5 4 3 2

INTRODUCTION

Welcome to the special Centennial Edition of "Ripley's Believe It or Not!", the most famous and best known entertainment feature in the world. The centennial series is designed to help celebrate the forthcoming hundredth anniversary of Robert L. Ripley's birth in 1993.

Ripley was one of the most fabulous and interesting personalities of the 20th century. He spent his life traveling the globe in pursuit of the odd, bizarre, and incredible-but-true stories that have filled the "Believe It or Not!" pages for over 70 years. During this period, more than 80 million people in 125 countries have been entertained and amazed by Robert L. Ripley's creation. In addition, millions more have marveled at the incredible oddities on display at the Ripley's museums in America, England, Canada, Australia, and Japan.

Ripley's amazing worldwide industry is a true American success story, for it started humbly with one man and an idea.

In 1918, the twenty-five-year-old Ripley was a hard-working sports cartoonist for the New York Globe newspaper. It happened one day that he was stuck for a cartoon to draw. As his daily deadline approached, he was still staring at a blank sheet on his drawing board when inspiration struck. Ripley dug into his files where he kept notes on all sorts of unusual sports achievements. He quickly sketched nine of the more interesting and bizarre items onto his page, and a legend was born. That first page was titled "Champs and Chumps." Ripley's editor quickly came up with a snappier name, and "Believe It or Not!" became an overnight sensation.

In 1929, Ripley published his very first collection of "Believe It or Not!" in book form. It was an immediate success. A few years later his feature was appearing in over 200 newspapers in the United States and Canada alone. But Ripley was just getting started. With financial backing from his newspaper syndicate, Ripley traveled thousands of miles in the next few years. He visited 198 countries, bringing back oddities, antiques, and amazing stories from each place he stopped. The best of these eventually wound up in his famous syndicated feature. The amazing truth is that Ripley supplied at least one "Believe It or Not!" every day for thirty years!

In 1933, Ripley collected many of his fabulous treasures and put them on exhibition in Chicago. Within a year, his "Odditorium" had hosted almost two and a half million people. They lined up around the block to see the displays of shrunken heads, postage-stamp-size paintings, treasures from the Orient, incredibly intricate matchstick models, and wickedly gleaming instruments of medieval torture.

Soon after Ripley died in 1949, his unique collection of oddities was gathered and displayed in the first permanent "Believe It or Not!" museum in St. Augustine, Florida. And, fittingly, Ripley himself became one of its more amazing items. A full-size replica of the man stood at the door, greeting all visitors and giving them a foretaste of the astonishing objects they would see inside.

Although Robert L. Ripley passed away, his work lives on. The Ripley's organization has ceaselessly provided daily "Believe It or Not!" pages through the decades, always reaching a bit farther for those fantastic (but true) stories that stretch the imagination. And they are still actively seeking more. If you know of any amazing oddity, write it down and send it in to:

Ripley's Believe It or Not!
90 Eglinton Avenue East, Suite 510
Toronto, Canada
M4P 2Y3

There are now over 110,000 "Believe it or Not!" cartoons that have been printed in over 300 categories. These include everything from amazing animals to catastrophes to *Reptiles, Lizards and Prehistoric Beasts,* the volume you hold right now. So sit back, get comfortable, and prepare to be astonished, surprised, amazed and delighted. Believe it or not!

A **HUGE TORTOISE**
IN PORT LOUIS,
ON THE
ISLAND OF
MAURITIUS,
*WALKED WITH 6
MEN ON
ITS BACK* 1850

THE TUATARA of New Zealand,
CALLED "THE LITTLE DRAGON," IS THE LAST SURVIVOR
OF THE AGE OF GIGANTIC DINOSAURS ··· YET FULLY
GROWN, IT IS ONLY 2 FEET LONG !

SCIENTISTS IN COLORADO RECENTLY DISCOVERED THE REMAINS OF "EPANTERIAS AMPLEXUS" A 50 FT.-LONG DINOSAUR WITH JAWS SO IMMENSE THAT IT COULD **SWALLOW PREY** THE SIZE OF A COW!

APOROSCELIS

A REPTILE OF SOMALILAND, IS CALLED "ASHERBODY," MEANING "BABY," *BECAUSE WHEN TOUCHED, IT MAKES A SOUND LIKE A CRYING INFANT*

THE COLORADO RIVER TOAD (*Bufo alvarius*) IS NO. AMERICA'S MOST POISONOUS TOAD... ITS VENOM CAN CAUSE PARALYSIS, SLURRED SPEECH, CONVULSIONS AND *EVEN DEATH !*

RATTLESNAKES

are not immune to one another's venom

THE CAMEROON HORNED TOAD
of Africa, IS PROTECTED FROM ITS HEAD TO ITS UPPER BACK BY A BONY CALCIUM SHIELD THAT RESEMBLES A *SUIT OF ARMOR*

I'M JUST A SOFTIE

THE **SHELL** OF A TURTLE TAKES MORE THAN A YEAR TO HARDEN

The
BALL
PYTHON

A SNAKE
4½ FEET LONG
AND 7 INCHES IN GIRTH
CAN BE HELD IN THE
PALM OF YOUR HAND!

PRESIDENT JOHN QUINCY ADAMS KEPT AN ALLIGATOR IN THE EAST ROOM OF THE WHITE HOUSE.

THE GIGANTOSAURUS
A HUGE AQUATIC REPTILE OF PREHISTORIC TIMES, WHEN STRETCHED ON ITS BELLY WAS 12 FEET HIGH, WITH A HEAD AND NECK 40 FEET LONG AND A TAIL 80 FEET IN LENGTH!

THE KOMODO DRAGON

of Indonesia,
THE WORLD'S LARGEST
LIZARD, GROWS UP TO
10 FEET IN LENGTH, CHARGES
AT GREAT SPEED AND HAS
BEEN KNOWN TO
DEVOUR HUMANS

THE **DINOSAUR**
AND TODAY'S BIRDS
ARE OFTEN DIRECTLY
RELATED, WITH THE BIRDS'
MUSCLES MUCH LIKE THOSE
OF THE PREHISTORIC BEAST...
TO BEST UNDERSTAND A
DINOSAUR'S ANATOMY, LOOK AT
THE BONES OF A CHICKEN

**THE MAN WHO WAS STRONGER
THAN A CROCODILE**

MOOSA A NATIVE OF TAMATAVE,
MADAGASCAR, WITH HIS LEG IN
THE JAWS OF A CROCODILE, SEIZED
THE REPTILE'S OWN LEG AND WON
HIS FREEDOM AND LIFE AFTER A
TUG OF WAR THAT LASTED A FULL HOUR

THE TRUNKBACK TURTLE
OFTEN ATTAINS A LENGTH OF **7** FEET
AND A WEIGHT OF 1,500 LBS. —YET IT
*CAN SWIM 100 YARDS IN LESS
THAN 10 SECONDS*

MIDWIFE TOAD
(Alytes obstetricans)

WHICH HATCHES ITS YOUNG BY WINDING A STRING OF EGGS AROUND ITS HIND LEGS

IS A MALE

EYEBALL TO EYEBALL

THE HORNED TOAD OF MEXICO AND SOUTHERN U.S. DESERTS, REACTS TO ATTACK BY *SQUIRTING BLOOD FROM ITS EYES AS FAR AS 5 FEET*

THE **AMPHIBIOUS TURTLE** IS THE ONLY CREATURE THAT HAS SURVIVED IN ALMOST ITS ORIGINAL FORM FOR OVER 200,000,000 YEARS

THE
**LARGEST
AMPHIBIAN
IN NATURE**
THE GIANT SALAMANDER of Japan
ATTAINS A LENGTH OF 5 FEET

IN 1922, SCIENTISTS IN MONGOLIA DISCOVERED INTACT *A NEST OF 18 PROTOCERATOP EGGS* FROM THE *MESOZOIC AGE OF DINOSAURS!*

THE CREATURE THAT CAN TREAD ON WATER
THE BASILISK, A LIZARD OF SO. AND CENT. AMERICA, *CAN RUN AS FAR AS ¼ OF A MILE ON THE SURFACE OF A LAKE OR POND*

BELIEVE IT OR *NOT!*
ONE THOUSAND TOADS
ONCE FELL FROM THE
SKY OVER A VILLAGE
IN FRANCE!

JACKSON'S CHAMELEON
of E. Africa, CHANGES COLOR BECAUSE ITS SKIN CONTAINS MELANIN *THE SUBSTANCE THAT ENABLES HUMAN SKIN TO TAN*

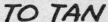

THE ALLIGATOR TURTLE CATCHES FISH WHEN THEY SEIZE ITS TONGUE--WHICH THEY MISTAKE FOR A WORM

THE SEA TURTLE HAS SUCH A HIGH MORTALITY RATE THAT ONLY ONE OUT OF EVERY 100 EGGS IT LAYS LIVES FOR A YEAR AND ONE OUT OF 1,000 EGGS REACHES ADULTHOOD

THE KING COBRA
LONGEST OF ALL POISONOUS SNAKES, REACHES A LENGTH OF 18 FEET. ITS DEADLY VENOM CAN KILL A MAN IN 20 MINUTES AND CAN EVEN KILL AN ELEPHANT IF IT STRIKES IN VULNERABLE PLACES ...*YET ALTHOUGH ASIANS FEAR ITS POISONOUS BITE, IT IS WORSHIPPED FROM INDIA TO INDONESIA*

THE TURTLE
HAS NOT CHANGED IN
200,000,000 YEARS

THE SURINAM TOAD
HAS NO TONGUE AND IS LESS
THAN AN INCH THICK

AN **ADULT TREE FROG** CAN JUMP 20 TIMES HIGHER THAN ITS BODY LENGTH

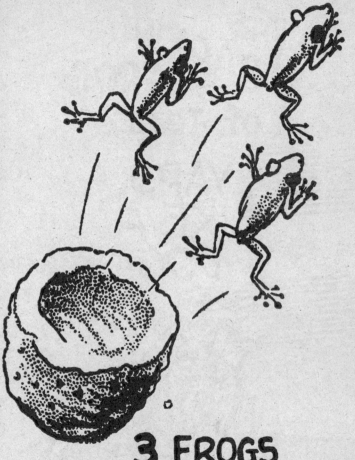

3 FROGS WERE FOUND IN A *POTATO !*

THE BARKING FROG

of Texas

YAPS LIKE A DOG

BELIEVE IT OR NOT!
SALAMANDERS
USE MUSCLES
IN THEIR LEGS
TO HEAR!

CROCODILES
BECAUSE OF THE WAY
THEY SHUFFLED ALONG,
WERE NAMED BY THE ANCIENT
GREEKS "KROKO-DRILOS,"
MEANING *"PEBBLE-WORMS"*

FROGS
NUMBER
ALMOST
3,000
SPECIES
-- *MOST OF WHICH
HAVE AN EXTERNAL
EARDRUM BEHIND
EACH EYE*

THE **TONGUE** OF THE DWARF FOUR-TOED SALAMANDER OF GEORGIA IS MOUNTED ON A STALK GROWING FROM ITS LOWER JAW

THE FLAT SNAKE
— A SEA SNAKE OF MALAYSIA

THE **GILA MONSTER** IS NORTH AMERICA'S ONLY *POISONOUS LIZARD*

THE MALE NOSE FROG NAMED FOR ITS ELONGATED SNOUT *HATCHES ITS EGGS IN ITS LARYNX*

THE PRINCIPLE OF MODERN BRIDGE BUILDING
COPIED FROM THE HINGED VERTEBRAE OF THE DINOSAURIAN OF 160,000,000 YEARS AGO.
*THE BONES IN THE BACK OF THIS ANIMAL ARE A MARVEL OF CONSTRUCTION
-ATTAINING A MAXIMUM OF STRENGTH WITH A MINIMUM OF WEIGHT*

TURTLE WITH GRASS GROWING ON ITS BACK

THE SEX OF A BOX TURTLE CAN BE DETERMINED BY THE COLOR OF ITS EYES

WEIRD HARROLD
WINNER OF THE 1984 CALAVERAS COUNTY JUMPING FROG CONTEST, IS ONLY 4½ INCHES LONG, BUT SET A WORLD RECORD WITH A 256½ INCH LEAP--OVER 57 TIMES HIS LENGTH!

OPPOSITES ATTRACT
THE MAJORITY OF WATER TURTLES EAT ANIMALS, BUT MOST LAND TURTLES EAT PLANTS

The THORNY-TAILED LIZARD *NEVER* DRINKS WATER

THE **BRAZILIAN CATFROG** CLIMBS A TREE THAT EXTENDS OVER WATER AND FORMS A LEAF INTO THE SHAPE OF A CONE *-IN WHICH THE FEMALE LAYS HER EGGS*

WHEN THE YOUNG EMERGE FROM THE EGGS THEY FALL DIRECTLY INTO THE WATER

THE SEVERED HEAD OF A RATTLESNAKE CAN STILL BITE AND INJECT VENOM FOR OVER 20 MINUTES

SNAKE-NECKED TURTLE
of AUSTRALIA HAS A NECK
TOO LONG TO BE DRAWN INTO ITS SHELL
— IT MUST BE FOLDED SIDEWAYS

THE **BEARDED AGAMA**
of Australia,   ACTUALLY HAS NO BEARD
IT PUFFS UP THE SPINY SKIN ON ITS THROAT
TO LOOK LIKE WHISKERS TO FRIGHTEN AWAY PREDATORS

THE MATAMATA TURTLE
OF BRAZIL'S AMAZON BASIN, IS HEAVILY ARMORED, HAS SPIKES ON ITS SHELL AND IMMOBILIZES ITS PREY BY SPITTING A PARALYZING SOLUTION AT IT

A **BLIND AMPHIBIAN SALAMANDER** (PROTEUS ANGUINUS)
FOUND IN SUBTERRANEAN CAVES IN CARNIOLA, YUGOSLAVIA,
CAN EITHER LAY EGGS OR BEAR LIVE LARVA

THE "DINOSAUR MAN"
STENONYCHOSAURUS INEQUALIS
a small meat-eating dinosaur, if it had not become extinct some
63,000,000 years ago, according to scientists at Canada's Nat.
Museum of Natural Sciences at Ottawa, would very probably
have evolved into a manlike creature 4½ feet tall, with a
large brain, green skin, and yellow reptilian eyes

THE **KING SNAKE**
DOES NOT HARM HUMANS
BUT KILLS AND EATS
*RATTLESNAKES AND
COPPERHEADS*

The
SEVERED HEAD OF A
TURTLE KILLED A CHICKEN

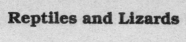

THE
DESERT NIGHT LIZARD
(Xantusia)
TO DISTRACT AN ATTACKER
SHEDS ITS TAIL

THE CRAWLING TREE

A TREE GREW ON THE
DIRT-COVERED BACK
OF A VERY OLD
AND VERY LARGE
ALLIGATOR

THE AGE OF A
RATTLESNAKE
IS _NOT_ COMPUTED BY
THE NUMBER OF ITS
RATTLES!

A RATTLER MAY GROW
2 TO 4 BUTTONS
A YEAR!

A VIPER BIT THE GRANDFATHER AND THE FANG REMAINED IN HIS BOOT. HIS SON AND GRANDSON WORE THE BOOTS AND WERE POISONED ALSO

ONE SNAKE BITE KILLED 3 GENERATIONS OF THE SAME FAMILY

THE **HUMERUS**
OF THE 160-FOOT-
LONG DINOSAUR
GIGANTOSAURUS
AFRICANUS, WAS
LARGER THAN A 6-
FOOT MAN--YET ITS
BRAIN WAS SMALLER
THAN A MAN'S FIST

THE **TOAD FROG** of Australia
WHEN THREATENED BY A SNAKE
*PUFFS ITSELF UP LIKE A TOY BALLOON
AND FLOATS SAFELY AWAY*

FROG
PREVENTED ITSELF FROM BEING
DEVOURED BY A WATER MOCCASIN
BY *GRASPING A STICK IN ITS MOUTH!*

A FROG
DOES *NOT* DRINK WATER
— It absorbs it

HARD-SHELLED TURTLES
LAY SOFT-SHELLED EGGS
SOFT-SHELLED TORTOISES
LAY HARD-SHELLED EGGS

SNAKES HAVE HIPS !

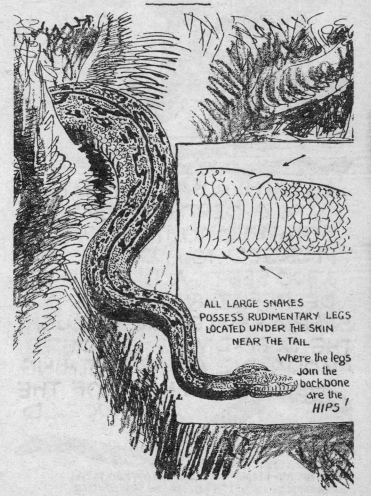

ALL LARGE SNAKES
POSSESS RUDIMENTARY LEGS
LOCATED UNDER THE SKIN
NEAR THE TAIL

Where the legs
join the
backbone
are the
HIPS !

A LEATHERBACK TURTLE
WITH A DEPTH RECORDER STRAPPED TO ITS BACK, PLUNGED TO A DEPTH OF 3,900 FEET--A DEPTH DEEPER THAN THAT OF A SPERM WHALE, LONG THOUGHT THE DEEP-DIVING LEADER AMONG THE AIR-BREATHING ANIMALS OF THE WORLD

THE TWO-HEADED BLIND SNAKE -Brazil
IS NEITHER A SNAKE - NOR BLIND
AND IS *NOT* TWO-HEADED – ALTHOUGH IT IS DIFFICULT TO TELL
WHICH END IS THE HEAD - IT IS A LIZARD - THE SAME DIAMETER
THROUGHOUT - AND CAN MOVE BACKWARD AND FORWARD AT WILL
IT LIVES IN ANT NESTS.!

THE WOMAN WHO WAS RESCUED BY A TURTLE!

MRS. CANDELARIA VILLANUEVA THROWN INTO THE SEA WHEN AN INTER-ISLAND PHILIPPINE PASSENGER SHIP SANK 600 MILES SOUTH OF MANILA, WAS KEPT AFLOAT FOR 2 DAYS BY A *GIANT SEA TURTLE!* MRS. VILLANUEVA WAS RIDING THE TURTLE'S BACK WHEN SHE WAS SIGHTED BY A RESCUE SHIP

THE AFRICAN RIDGEBACK FROG
of Equatorial Africa, LAYS EGGS
THAT HATCH IN LESS THAN A DAY
AND A HALF CONTRASTED TO
NEARLY TWO WEEKS FOR THOSE
IN COOLER CLIMATES

THE ORNITHOLESTES
A DINOSAUR ONLY 6 FEET LONG
WEIGHED LITTLE MORE THAN A TURKEY

JAMES "DINOSAUR JIM" JENSEN

a paleontologist of Brigham Young University in Provo, Utah, has in 30 years collected more than *100 TONS OF FOSSIL BONES!*

THE ARCHELON, A GIANT SEA-TURTLE THAT LIVED 80 MILLION YEARS AGO, WAS THE SIZE OF THREE PING-PONG TABLES.

THE FROG IS UNAWARE WHEN CHANGES IN ITS BODY OCCUR GRADUALLY---SO LONG AS IT IS NOT DONE SUDDENLY, IT CAN BE FROZEN TO DEATH OR ROASTED WITHOUT VISIBLE DISCOMFORT

SNAKES in the mountains of Valais, Switzerland, LIE ON THE SHORES OF MOUNTAIN STREAMS AND SEIZE TROUT WHEN THEY LEAP ABOVE THE WATER

A HIGHWAY

IN SHAWNEE NATIONAL FOREST IN
SOUTHERN ILLINOIS IS CLOSED TO ALL
AUTOMOBILES FOR SEVERAL WEEKS
TWICE EACH YEAR SO IT CAN BE
*CROSSED SAFELY BY COPPERHEADS,
RATTLESNAKES AND WATER MOCCASINS*

SOUTH AMERICAN
HORNED FROG
HAS TEETH AND BARKS LIKE A DOG!

FLYING SNAKE
of JAVA

A RARE AND REMARKABLE SPECIES THAT
FLATTENS OUT LIKE A RIBBON AND SAILS
FROM TREE TO TREE.

A TURTLE CLOSES ITS EYES
FROM THE BOTTOM

MUSIC HATH CHARMS
TO SOOTHE
THE SAVAGE BREAST?
NO!
SNAKES CAN'T HEAR!

Women **SNAKE WORSHIPERS** of Dahomey, Africa, ARE OBLIGED TO PICK UP EVERY SNAKE THEY ENCOUNTER AND TRANSPORT IT TO THE NEAREST TEMPLE — *WOUND AROUND THEIR NECK LIKE A NECKLACE*

THE GOLIATH FROG
(Rana goliath)
FOUND ONLY IN THE CAMEROONS, IS A FOOT LONG

THE SEA SNAKE
AFTER EATING A FISH WITH SPINES EJECTS THE SPINES THROUGH ITS BODY WALLS

THE WHIPTAIL LIZARDS
of Southwestern United States
ARE ALL FEMALES

A "**DRAGON'S SKULL**" LONG EXHIBITED IN THE CHURCH OF MONS, BELGIUM, IN THE BELIEF IT WAS THAT OF A DRAGON SLAIN IN THE CRUSADES HAS BEEN IDENTIFIED *AS THAT OF A CROCODILE*

A SNAKE TIED ITSELF INTO A KNOT
TO *CURE* A *BROKEN BACK*

TORTOISE SHELL
DOES **NOT** COME FROM TORTOISES

IT COMES FROM THE SEA TURTLE AND ALSO CAN BE MADE SYNTHETICALLY

the **TUATARA** Primitive Reptile of New Zealand
HAS A *THIRD* EYE ON TOP OF ITS HEAD!

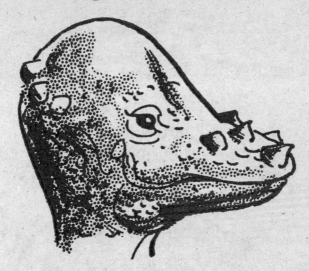

PACHYCEPHAL-OSAURUS

A PREHISTORIC
DINOSAUR
HAD A SKULL
26 INCHES LONG
AND 9 INCHES THICK

THE GECKO
the only lizard with a voice,
when startled says, *"EEK"*

The
TORTOISE HAS THE SLOWEST PULSE BEAT OF ANY ANIMAL
13 PULSATIONS A MINUTE

IT'S AGAINST THE LAW
IN DETROIT, MICH., TO TIE YOUR
CROCODILE TO A FIRE HYDRANT

THE KING COBRA HAS VENOM SO DEADLY, THAT ONE GRAM COULD KILL 150 PERSONS

THE SANDFISH
IS NOT A FISH
IT IS A LIZARD THAT SEALS
ITS EAR OPENINGS BEFORE
BURYING ITSELF IN THE SANDS
OF THE SAHARA DESERT

TURTLES
IN PAPUA, NEW GUINEA,
COME ASHORE EVERY DECEMBER
TO LAY THEIR EGGS. THE AEK-
YOM PEOPLE COUNT THE
YEARS AND THEIR AGES
BY THE TIMES THE
TURTLES LEAVE THE
SEA FOR THE LAND

AN **ALLIGATOR**
CAN RUN AS *FAST AS A HORSE*!

The GIANT LIZARDS OF KOMODO
Dutch East Indies
ARE DEAF!

THE BASILISK of Panama,
A LIZARD 3 FEET LONG, HAS FEET THAT ARE
NOT WEBBED - *YET IT RUNS ON WATER!*

The **TURTLE** IS THE ONLY
ANIMAL THAT HAS ITS HIP
BONES AND SHOULDER BONES
INSIDE THE RIB CAGE

THE STICKY TONGUE OF THE CHAMELEON
EXTENDS UP TO 1½ TIMES ITS BODY LENGTH
TO CAPTURE AN INSECT AND ZIP IT INTO ITS MOUTH
···*ALL WITHIN ONE-TENTH OF A SECOND*

THE SMOKY JUNGLE FROG
of the So. American jungles, WEIGHS ONLY ONE POUND -YET IT CAN SWALLOW A SNAKE 4½ FEET LONG

CROCODILES and **ALLIGATORS** ARE THE ONLY REPTILES WITH **LOUD VOICES**

YOU DON'T HAVE TO SHOUT!

THE **SPRING PEEPER**

THE SMALLEST OF ALL FROGS, MEASURING ONLY ONE INCH

"MOKELE-MBEMBE"

A DINOSAUR-LIKE BEAST, HAS BEEN SIGHTED SEVERAL TIMES IN THE AFRICAN CONGO'S LAKE TELLE AREA BY MANY PEOPLE, INCLUDING MEMBERS OF A SCIENTIFIC EXPEDITION -- ACCORDING TO THE SCIENTISTS IT COULD BE THE WORLD'S LAST SURVIVING DINOSAUR!

JON BEDFORD

OF NEW MEXICO HAS CREATED LIFE-SIZE SCULPTURES—INCLUDING AN ANACONDA, A RHINOCEROS AND A STEGOSAURUS—MADE FROM THE CHROME BUMPERS OF OLD CARS!

LUCKY

A 25-YEAR-OLD, 350LB.
SEA TURTLE WHOSE
FLIPPERS WERE SLASHED
OFF BY A SHARK IN
THE FLORIDA KEYS, WAS
*GIVEN ARTIFICIAL
FLIPPERS IN A
3½ HOUR OPERATION*
AT ISLAMORADA, FLA.

A RATTLESNAKE
WILL DIE IF LEFT
IN THE HOT SUN
20 MINUTES

THE JURY
IN ALL
CRIMINAL CASES
in the Bangangte Tribe,
Africa
IS A TORTOISE!
*IT CONVICTS THE DEFENDANT BY
MOVING TOWARD THE JUDGE—
FREES HIM BY TURNING IN THE
OPPOSITE DIRECTION*

THE **HELMETED LIZARD** of Central America

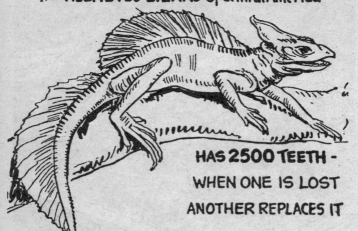

HAS **2500 TEETH** –

WHEN ONE IS LOST

ANOTHER REPLACES IT

MALE CRICKET FROGS OF SOUTH AMERICA HAVE SUCH LARGE VOCAL SACS THAT THEY CARRY THEIR EGGS TO TERM *INSIDE THE POUCHES.!*

A REPTILE

active during the daytime has
eyes with round pupils—while
those active at night
have slitlike pupils

THE WALKING DESALINIZATION PLANT

THE CHUCKWALLA of Arizona, DURING PROLONGED DRY SPELLS *DRINKS SALT WATER WHICH IT CAN CONVERT INTO FRESH WATER*

THE HEART OF A TURTLE

IN WARM SUMMER WATER BEATS UP TO 40 TIMES A MINUTE, BUT IN WINTER WHEN IT ALMOST SUSPENDS ANIMATION IN COLD WATER, THE HEART BEATS ONLY ONCE IN **10** MINUTES

THE
FLYING DRAGON
IS A LIZARD,
WITH ELONGATED
RIBS COVERED WITH
DILATANT SKIN
IT SAILS
FROM TREE
TO TREE

BUILT-IN HEATING AND AIR CONDITIONING DIMETRODON

a pelycosaur that lived
300,000,000 years ago,
had a large dorsal sail that
absorbed sunlight,
CHANGING DIRECTION FOR COOLING

THE THERAPSIDA

a tiny reptile that lived
225,000,000 years ago in the
age of the dinosaurs, evolved
into today's mammals — and, say
scientists, is the
ANCESTOR OF EVERY HUMAN

THE
SOUTH AMERICAN
TREE FROG
(Nototrema Marsupiatum)
CARRIES ITS EGGS
IN A POUCH
ON ITS BACK

THE ANCIENT PLESIOSAUR

a gigantic marine animal, swallowed rocks weighing as
much as 20 pounds — for ballast while swimming!

THE SURINAM TOAD
(Pipa Americana)
of Brazil
HATCHES 100 EGGS
FROM HOLES IN ITS BACK

THE TREE TOAD of MARTINIQUE CLIMBS TREES WITH ITS YOUNG *CLINGING TO ITS BACK BY SUCTION CUPS*

BELIEVE IT OR NOT! A DESERT TORTOISE CAN LIVE FOR A WHOLE YEAR *ON WHAT A COW EATS IN A SINGLE DAY!*

THE TANYSTROPHEUS, A REPTILE THAT LIVED 22 MILLION YEARS AGO IN EUROPE, HAD A 13-FT.-LONG NECK *THAT WAS TWICE AS LONG AS ITS BODY!*

THE TINY COQUI FROG OF PUERTO RICO, HAS A LONG NAME, ILEUTHIRODACTYLUS COQUI, BUT IS UNDER TWO INCHES IN LENGTH AND WEIGHS BUT 3/10THS OF AN OUNCE WHEN WET--YET ITS 108-DECIBEL CALL IS MORE EAR SPLITTING THAN A SUBWAY TRAIN OR A LOW-FLYING JET

CROCODILES
FOUND IN THE
SHARI RIVER,
AFRICA,
*ARE STRIPED
LIKE ZEBRAS*

THE TREE FROG
of Borneo BUILDS A NEST FOR
ITS EGGS OUT OF 2 LEAVES
WHICH IT FASTENS TOGETHER
*BY A FOAM IT WHIPS UP
OUT OF VEGETATION*

THE BLOOD CELLS OF A FROG ARE 5 TIMES AS LARGE AS THOSE OF AN ELEPHANT!

THE MOZAMBIQUE SPITTING COBRA
ONE OF AFRICA'S MOST DANGEROUS REPTILES, WHEN THREATENED, WILL REAR UP AND SPIT TWO DEADLY STREAMS OF VENOM **UP TO 9 FEET AT THE FACE OR EYES OF ITS ENEMY**

THE ARROW-POISON FROG

(DENDROBATES TYPOGRAPHUS)

SECRETES IN ITS BACK A VENOM INTO WHICH SOUTH AMERICAN INDIANS *DIP BLOWGUN DARTS*

A FROG WILL SUFFOCATE IF ITS MOUTH IS HELD OPEN
It Must <u>Swallow</u> Air

A **LIZARD** SMELLS THROUGH ITS FORKED TONGUE

THE **TREE FROG**
of the W. Indies
LIVES IN
TREETOPS
AND EVEN
LAYS ITS
EGGS IN THE
BRANCHES
OF A TREE

THE

PLATANNA
a frog of South Africa
CAN JUMP BOTH FORWARD AND BACKWARD ON LAND OR IN THE WATER

THE FEMALE AMERICAN ALLIGATOR
TO START A COURTSHIP, SWIMS IN FRONT OF A
MALE TO BLOCK HIS PATH OR PRODS HIM WITH
HER SNOUT TO MAKE HIM SWIM IN THE
DIRECTION SHE WANTS

The "OSTRICH" FROG

THE WESTERN FROG AT THE FIRST SIGN OF DANGER BURIES ITS HEAD IN THE MUD

THE **KEMP'S RIDLEY TURTLE**
SMALLEST AND RAREST OF
THE SEA TURTLES IS SO SCARCE
THAT THE MEXICAN GOVERNMENT
*SENT MARINES TO GUARD
THE ONLY BEACH ON
WHICH IT
NESTS*

A SKELETON
OF THE WORLD'S
LONGEST DINOSAUR,
THE 150,000,000-
YEAR-OLD DIPLODOCUS,
EXHIBITED AT THE
CARNEGIE MUSEUM
OF NATURAL HISTORY
IN PITTSBURGH, PA.,
IS OVER **84**
FEET LONG

THE VOICE OF THE TURTLE —

THE WOOD TURTLE HAS A WHISTLE THAT CAN BE HEARD 40 FEET AWAY

TOROSAURUS WAS A HORNED DINOSAUR WITH A FRILLED BONE AT ITS NECK AND A HEAD **THE SIZE OF A SMALL CAR.!**

"CROATI"

a 15-pound rattlesnake at Louisiana College is over 30 years old, the oldest-known in captivity, and is kept healthy according to C.J. Cavanaugh, professor emeritus of biology, *BY BEING FED ONLY 3 TIMES A YEAR!*

THE "PARROT LIZARD"
(Psittacosaurus) FOUND IN
PREHISTORIC MONGOLIA
AND CHINA 110,000,000
YEARS AGO, SURVIVED
ON VEGETATION WHICH
IT GRASPED IN ITS
"HANDS" AND ATE
WITH A BEAK
RESEMBLING
A PARROT'S

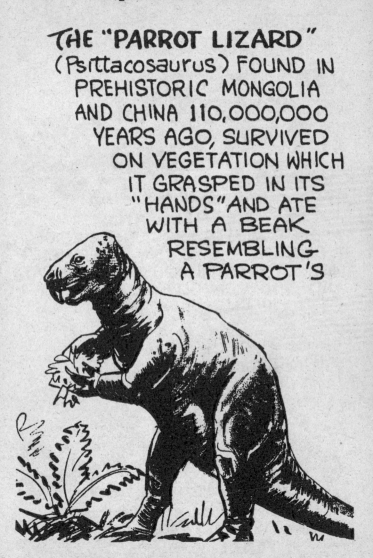

THE ALLIGATOR
WHOSE BRAIN IS ABOUT THE SIZE OF
A POKER CHIP, CAN STAY UNDER WATER
WITHOUT BREATHING FOR A FULL DAY
AND CAN EVEN GO FOR A FULL YEAR
WITHOUT EATING

THE PREHISTORIC STEGOSAURUS
HAD A BRAIN THE SIZE OF A GOLF BALL AND ONE OR TWO
ROWS OF LARGE BONY PLATES ON ITS BACK USED FOR
DEFENSE AND TO REGULATE ITS BODY TEMPERATURE

THE BLINDWORM
IS ALSO CALLED THE SLOWWORM AND THE DEAF ADDER
-YET IT IS NOT BLIND NOR SLOW NOR DEAF NOR IS IT AN ADDER NOR A WORM
IT IS A LEGLESS LIZARD

JEFF GRAY
of Port Neches, Texas,
HEARING A STRANGE NOISE,
OPENED THE HOOD OF HIS
CAR AND FOUND A 5-FOOT
ALLIGATOR ATOP HIS ENGINE

THE FIRST WHOLE DINOSAUR EGGS
EVER FOUND IN NO. AMERICA
WERE DISCOVERED IN
MONTANA ON JULY 12, 1979

SNAKES SHED THEIR SKIN 3 TO 6 TIMES EACH YEAR!

THE THORNY DEVIL

(Moloch horridus) of Australia, IS PROTECTED BY ITS SHARP SPIKES... IT EATS 1,800 ANTS AT ONE TIME AND STORES WATER IN CANALS INTER-SECTING ITS SCALES WHICH LEAD TO ITS MOUTH

GIGANTIC TORTOISES of the Galapagos Islands BATTLE ONLY BY SYMBOLICALLY BUMPING NOSES -- OR CHARGING EACH OTHER WITH THEIR HEADS WITHDRAWN INSIDE THEIR SHELLS

SNAKES HAVE NO
EXTERNAL EARS

THEY TUNE "IN" ON THE
SOUND WAVES WITH
THEIR TONGUES

THE SYMBOL IN W. Africa FOR ETERNITY IS A SNAKE *BITING ITS OWN TAIL*

A SNAKE SLEEPS WITH BOTH EYES OPEN

COUCH'S SPADEFOOT TOAD

found in No. America's Sonoran desert, lives underground 11 months each year, surfacing only during the July rainy season — yet during those two to four weeks it *EATS ENOUGH TO LAST IT FOR 11 MONTHS*

THE
FRILLED LIZARD
of Australia
STORES THE
INSECTS
IT FEEDS
UPON
IN THE
FOLDS
OF ITS
HUGE
COLLAR

HAIRY TORTOISES
FOUND ONLY IN ONE LAKE IN KIANG-SI , CHINA

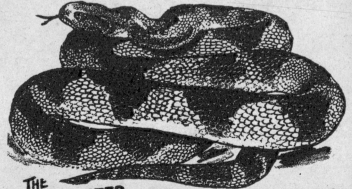

THE **BUSHMASTER** - MOST DEADLY SNAKE ! GROWS TO 12 FT IN LENGTH

SAFFRON CROCUS
GAVE THE CROCODILE ITS NAME BECAUSE THE ANCIENTS BELIEVED THAT WHEN IT INHALED THE FLOWER'S FRAGRANCE *THE CROCODILE SHED REAL TEARS OF PLEASURE*

THE NILE CROCODILE IS THE ONLY ANIMAL IN NATURE THAT MAKES AUDIBLE SOUNDS WHILE IT IS STILL *IN ITS EGG*

THE EGG IS BURIED IN THE GROUND, AND THE YOUNG CROCODILE'S "HONK" IS A SIGNAL TO ITS PARENT THAT IT IS TIME TO DIG UP THE EGG

IN 1894, **D**URING A SEVERE HAILSTORM IN BOVINA, MS, A 6" TURTLE ENCASED IN ICE FELL TO THE GROUND!

THE GREEN TREE FROG

IS A VENTRILOQUIST

IT THROWS ITS VOICE SO PREDATORS CAN NEVER LOCATE IT BY ITS CROAKING

KRONOSAURUS

A GIANT MONSTER OF PRE-
HISTORIC TIMES, EXISTED
100,000,000 YEARS AGO
IN THE SEA THAT COVERED
MUCH OF AUSTRALIA...
IT WAS 42 FT. LONG,
HAD A 9 FT. HEAD AND
IS THE LARGEST-KNOWN
FLESH-EATING
MARINE REPTILE

THE BARKING FROG

WHEN DISTURBED
INFLATES ITSELF
TO MANY TIMES
ITS NORMAL SIZE
*AND WAILS LIKE A
HUMAN INFANT*

THE **GIANT MARINE IGUANA** OF THE GALAPAGOS ISLANDS, IF DEPRIVED OF WATER FOR AS LONG AS 100 DAYS CAN *SURVIVE ON SALT WATER*

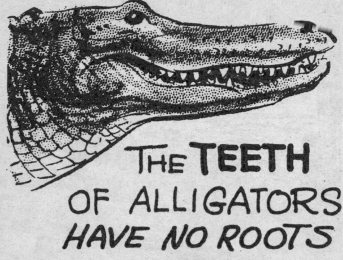

The **TEETH**
OF ALLIGATORS
HAVE NO ROOTS

A **DINOSAUR TRACK** FOUND IN A QUARRY AT GRANBY, MASS., BY ROUVILLE F. GINGRAS, *IS 59 INCHES LONG* ··· EXPERTS ESTIMATE THE ANIMAL MEASURED 70 FEET

A LIGHT LUNCH

A 4-FOOT PINE SNAKE
UNDERWENT SUCCESSFUL
SURGERY AT THE UNIV. OF
FLORIDA AT GAINSVILLE
IN AUG. 1986 FOR THE
REMOVAL OF TWO 15-
WATT LIGHT BULBS
WHICH IT HAD SWALLOWED

DURING THE FLORIDA
HURRICANE OF 1926 —
A 12-FOOT ALLIGATOR
WAS BLOWN OUT OF THE
WATER AND CARRIED
2 MILES IN THE AIR!

THE CHAMELEON

ACCORDING TO RECENT SCIENTIFIC
STUDIES, DOES NOT CHANGE COLOR TO
CAMOUFLAGE ITSELF BUT IN RESPONSE
TO LIGHT AND TEMPERATURE CHANGES--
AND TO EXPRESS ITS EMOTIONS

THE **CHAMELEON** HAS EYELIDS THAT COMPLETELY COVER ITS EYES EXCEPT FOR A TINY HOLE AND IT CAN *SIMULTANEOUSLY LOOK BOTH FORWARD AND BACKWARD*

THE **SALT-WATER CROCODILES** of Ceylon, OFTEN GROW TO A LENGTH OF **22 FEET,** AND WEIGH MORE THAN **1,600 POUNDS**

THE **AXOLOTL** a salamander **EATS MORE THAN ITS OWN WEIGHT IN A SINGLE MEAL**

THE **ZEBRA-TAILED LIZARD** PROTECTS ITS FEET FROM THE HOT DESERT SAND **BY TIPTOING**

A **TURTLE** WAS FOUND. ALIVE BENEATH **8** FEET OF SOLID ROCK College Station, Texas

IT WAS BURIED BY A ROCK SLIDE CENTURIES AGO AND DUG UP BY WORKMEN EXCAVATING FOR TEXAS A.&M. UNIVERSITY

FISH AND **REPTILES**
CONTINUE TO
GROW AS LONG
AS THEY LIVE

THE RETICULATED PYTHON
CAN SURVIVE FOR 679
DAYS WITHOUT FOOD.

A SNAKE SWALLOWED AN EGG
- CRAWLED THRU A KNOTHOLE
AND SWALLOWED ANOTHER
Thus MAKING ITSELF PRISONER

A FROG
MUST CLOSE ITS EYES TO SWALLOW

CYNOGNATHUS A MAMMAL-LIKE REPTILE THAT LIVED 180 MILLION YEARS AGO, WAS NEARLY 8 FEET LONG AND *HAD A SKULL AND JAWS LIKE THOSE OF A DOG*

THE
**HAIRY
FROG**
of Africa

IS
COVERED
WITH *FUR*
(Trichobatrachus robustus)

THE FIRST USE OF BIOLOGICAL AND PSYCHOLOGICAL WARFARE!

HANNIBAL

(247-183 B.C.) THE CARTHAGINIAN GENERAL ENABLED KING PRUSIAS OF BITHYNIA TO WIN A GREAT NAVAL VICTORY OVER KING EUMENES OF PERGAMUM BY SUGGESTING THAT THE BITHYNIANS HURL ONTO THE DECKS OF THE ENEMY'S SHIPS *EARTHENWARE JUGS FILLED WITH VENOMOUS SNAKES!*

THE ENTIRE CREW OF THE ENGLISH WARSHIP, "DAEDALUS," SAILING BETWEEN ST. HELENA AND THE CAPE OF GOOD HOPE REPORTED SIGHTING A *SEA SERPENT 65 FEET LONG AND EXTENDING 4 FEET ABOVE THE SEA* (August 6, 1848)

THE GREEN TREE FROG
(Hyla arborea)
USUALLY A BRILLIANT GREEN, CHANGES AT TIMES TO GREY, BLUE OR BLACK AND SHEDS ITS SKIN EVERY 14 DAYS

A MOTHER CROCODILE
TRANSPORTS HER BABIES IN HER MOUTH CARRYING THEM BEHIND HER HUGE TEETH AS IF SHE WAS ABOUT TO SWALLOW THEM

MALE AUSTRALIAN BROWN SNAKES

WHEN FIGHTING, WIND TOGETHER LIKE A DOUBLE-COILED ROPE AND SEPARATE ONLY WHEN BOTH ARE EXHAUSTED···THE LOSER THEN RETREATS

"BONEHEADS" THE PACHYCEPHALOSAURUS WAS A DINOSAUR WITH A *9-IN.-THICK SKULL* THAT ACTED LIKE A CRASH HELMET DURING FIGHTS

STENONYCHOSAURUS
A PREHISTORIC DINOSAUR, WAS ONLY 6½ FT. LONG — YET IT HAD A LARGE BRAIN AND WAS THE MOST INTELLIGENT OF ALL DINOSAURS

VISIT THESE RIPLEY'S MUSEUMS

Ripley's Believe It or Not! Museum
7850 Beach Blvd.
Buena Park, California 90620
(714) 522-7932

Ripley's Believe It or Not! Museum
175 Jefferson Street
San Francisco, California 94133
(415) 771-6188

Ripley Memorial Museum/Church of One Tree
492 Sonoma Avenue
Santa Rosa, California 95401
(707) 576-5233

Ripley's Believe It or Not! Museum
19 San Marco Avenue
St. Augustine, Florida 32084
(904) 824-1606

Ripley's Believe It or Not! Museum
202 East Fremont Street
Las Vegas, Nevada 89101
(702) 385-4011

Ripley's Believe It or Not! Museum
202 S.W. Bay Blvd.
Mariner Square
Newport, Oregon 97365
(503) 265-2206

Ripley's Believe It or Not! Museum
901 North Ocean Blvd.
Myrtle Beach, South Carolina 29578
(803) 448-2331

Ripley's Believe It or Not! Museum
800 Parkway
Gatlinburg, Tennesse 37738
(615) 436-5096

Ripley's Believe It or Not! Museum
301 Alamo Plaza (across from the Alamo)
San Antonio, Texas 78205
(512) 224-9299

Ripley's Believe It or Not! Museum
601 East Safari Parkway
Grand Prairie, Texas 75050
(214) 263-2391

Ripley's Believe It or Not! Museum
115 Broadway
Wisconsin Dells, Wisconsin 53965
(608) 254-2184

Ripley's Believe It or Not! Museum
P.O. Box B1
Raptis Plaza, Cavill Mall
Surfer's Paradise, Queensland
Australia 4217
(61) 7-592-0040

Ripley's Believe It or Not! Museum
Units 5 and 6
Ocean Boulevard, South Promenade
Blackpool, Lancashire
England

Ripley's Believe It or Not! Museum
Yong-In Farmland
310, Jeonda-Ri, Pogok-Myon
Yongin-Gun, Kyonggi-do, Korea

Ripley's Believe It or Not! Museum
Aunque Ud. No Lo Crea de Ripley
Londres No. 4
Col. Juarez
C.P. 06600 Mexico, D.F.

Ripley's Believe It or Not! Museum
4960 Clifton Hill
Niagara Falls, Ontario, L2G 3N4
(416) 356-2238

Ripley's Believe It or Not! Museum
Cranberry Village
Cavendish, P.E.I C0A 1N0
Canada
(902) 963-3444.